# Dowsing...

## for Answers and Healing

# Also by Vicky Thurlow

## Books
*Changing the Face of God*
*Affirmations to Change and Heal Your Life*

## Audio/CD
Guided Meditations:
*Experience Joy*
*Achieve Your Goals*
*Increase Confidence*
*Increase Love, Faith, and Trust*
*Increase Creativity and Self-Expression*
*Break Bad Habits and Addictions*
*Inner Peace, Security, and Spiritual Awakenings*
*Rest for the Mind, Body, and Sprit*
*Morning Meditation/Peaceful Sleep*
*Healing Meditation*
*Guided Meditation Series*

## Visual/DVD
*BreaThin—Effective Breathing Techniques*

For more information about Vicky Thurlow's work, books, guided meditations, CDs, DVDs, workshops, and healing resources, please visit her Web site, http://www.pursuitofhealing.com.

# Dowsing...

## for Answers and Healing
## Emotionally, Physcially, and Spiritually

# Vicky Thurlow

**DVT**

Grand Junction, Colorado

*This book is not intended as medical advice and the author does not dispense medical or psychological advice or prescribe the use of any technique as a form of treatment without the advice of a physician. The author's intent is to offer information in general to help in emotional, physical, and spiritual growth. The author assumes no responsibility for your actions should you choose to use any techniques or suggestions.*

Published by
DVT Investments
2800 Printers Way
Grand Junction, Colorado 81506

Publisher's Cataloging-in-Publication Data
Thurlow, Vicky.

   Dowsing for answers and healing : emotionally, physically, and spiritually /
   Vicky Thurlow. — Grand Junction, Colo. : DVT Investments, 2008.

   p. ; cm.

   ISBN: 978-0-9816480-3-3

   1. Self-actualization (Psychology) 2. Dowsing. 3. Mind and body.
   4. Well-being—Psychological aspects. I. Title.

   BF637.S4 T485 2008
   158—dc22                                                        2008928949

Project coordination by Jenkins Group, Inc
www.BookPublishing.com
Interior design by Brooke Camfield

Printed in the United States of America
by Colorado Printing Company, Grand Junction, Colorado
12  11  10  09  08  •  5  4  3  2  1

# CONTENTS

# Contents

# ACKNOWLEDGMENTS

One person in particular led me to this wonderful Universal gift, her name is Deborah Kinnes. Deborah is deeply spiritual, highly intuitive, and a dedicated healer using many wonderful techniques including acupuncture, Chinese herbs, Psych-K, flower essences, and dowsing. Words can hardly describe my gratitude for our meeting again in this lifetime. Thank you Deborah, for everything. May your passion for healing continue to bless others and you.

I also thank all of you who have asked and allowed me to use the gift of dowsing in your lives. There have been many. I have been greatly blessed to have facilitated and witnessed the finding of precious lost objects, the healing of relationships, the breaking of addictions, as well as miraculous healings. Each one of you has contributed in the building of my faith and abilities. I thank you for trusting me.

And to Jordan for being so brave and for agreeing to be such a great gift in this lifetime to so many people . . . especially me.

# INTRODUCTION

There isn't a person alive who hasn't wondered what to do in a certain situation. There isn't a person alive who hasn't gone ahead and made a decision only to find that it was the wrong one and then suffered greatly because of it. There isn't a person alive who has all the answers readily in their conscious mind. This, my friend, is where the gift of dowsing plays a part in our lives.

There are many alternative healing techniques that offer the knowledge and ability of working with the properties of Energy and each different technique offers its own unique way of accessing Universal information. Dowsing is just one technique that opens communication between our conscious, sub-conscious and unconscious minds. It is a very simple and effective way of working with Energy to access unlimited information and knowledge. It also offers a physical sign that Energy is moving. I consider it a Universal gift because it allows anyone who is open to it the ability to tap into a Higher-Self or God as some call it. Anyone who learns to tap in to Universal Energy has the ability to gain knowledge, answers, wisdom, and healing. There is an unlimited source of information and Power available to each one of us if we only take the time to learn and develop our skills using various techniques. If you are seeking healing and answers, your journey begins by finding a path or technique that allows you to tap into unlimited knowledge that will uplift, enlighten and heal not only yourself but those around you.

I was raised, as many other people have been, in a very mind-controlling religion. The Seventh Day Adventists Church never allowed for self trust or self-realization and, in fact, taught that everything good or bad, answers, hunches, illnesses, accidents, even miracles, all came from "out there" and was either the fault or blessing of God or the devil. I was taught that I, as an individual, had no Power. In addition to lack of trust in self (powerlessness), I lived with the constant threat of losing my salvation if I were to think beyond the doctrines or boundaries of the church. Religions or psychological abuse based on fear and guilt never allows a person to experience any type of thinking or trust from inside themselves. You are simply *taught or brainwashed into believing that something" out there" has all the Power . . . your Power*. If you believe everything comes from "out there," there is no way to trust your own feelings or intuition from inside. There are two beliefs about this: One is that everything is from God or the devil and they are "out there." The other belief is that all Power is "within" you.

If you have no belief or trust in yourself it is impossible for you to hear your own powerful intuition or your own voice. If your inner voice has been squelched by religion or other controlling beliefs it will be almost impossible for you to make the right choices and tough decisions about anything until you learn to hear that voice again. People who have no belief in themselves find they are in a vicious cycle of wanting God to give them answers from "out there" and . . . it never happens. Why? Because God doesn't live "out there." I write extensively about this in my book *Changing the Face of God*. In it, I teach why it's so important for you to *realize* that God or Universal Energy, or Spirit, is "within" you not "out there" and how to meet up with your Higher-Self. When you *realize* that healing and answers come from "within," you will begin to shift your search from outside to inside.

With discipline and practice you can learn to use various techniques that will assist you in hearing your inner voice, your intuition, Universal Energy, or your Higher Self. When you hear yourself you will begin to get all the healing and answers you desire.

The most difficult thing about finding answers from "within" is taking the time to find what techniques work best for you. If you take the time to learn, and you find yourself in a situation where you need to make an important or even a not so important decision, you will then have the ability to tap into all the answers you need. With the right tools you will be able to decide on the best college, a mate for life, the right school for your children, or on a house, car, a career move, all with complete confidence. I know what you're thinking. "Where do I find those tools?" I'm about to tell you.

I'm sure you have heard many people claim to pray to God "out there" for answers and he tells (or doesn't tell) them what to do. I respect their belief, but I personally don't believe it. I prayed to the Christian God for forty years of my life and he never once told me anything. But the very first time I dowsed, I immediately got an answer. The amazing thing was the answer came from me. It came from the Power "within" me. I had turned up the volume to my voice, my intuition, or Higher Self, by learning to use the gift of dowsing. God, Universe or Power as some call it, is not "out there" judging, condemning, and watching everything we do. It is an unlimited Energy source that is "inside" each and every one of us and is available to be used however we choose. Therein lies all of our wisdom, answers, healing, and happiness. Inside! Understanding that everything is connected energetically and that we are all one, will allow you to do amazing work. Just remember, dowsing, or Energy work, is not magic. It is the art of learning to direct Energy.

I must tell you that when I first began dowsing, there were many people who thought I had lost it or was working with the devil.

I'm pretty sure some people even thought I was some kind of nut. Whatever! Since that time, fortunately many of those same people have come to me for healing and answers and have had amazing and miraculous things happen in their lives. Those who continue to think I'm strange certainly have the right to do so. It does not change my belief in this wonderful gift and it most definitely does not keep me from sharing it with others. Be forewarned; you will definitely come across resistance from certain people when you begin to dowse. Choose wisely with whom you share your gift and your experiences. Sometimes silence is best.

Learning to dowse has not only allowed me to find healing, answers, and happiness for myself, it has allowed me to find healing and answers for many others. I have been blessed to witness everything from finding lost objects, to making good real estate decisions, right career moves, and miraculous healings. What I love most about dowsing is that it is simply a way to tap into what I already know. It's empowering beyond belief!

It's time now for you to empower your life and tap into what you already know. Let's begin.

# DAILY CHECK LIST

Am I in balance with earth Energy?

Is my aura balanced?

Are all my Chakras open and balanced?

Do I have any negative entities on or around me?

Do I have any non-beneficial frequencies on or around me?

Do I have any non-beneficial psychic cords?

Do I have any non-beneficial perceptions?

Do I have any curses, hexes, vexes, black magic, witchcraft, or bad medicine on me?

Use the chart for the following:

What is my life force?

What is my Energy level?

What is my body frequency?

What is my motivation level?

What is my compatibility level?

What is my prosperity level?

# DOWSING CHART

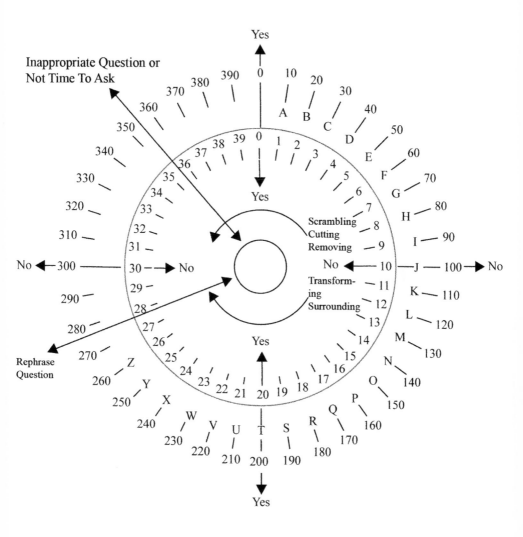

# CHAPTER 1

# WHAT IS DOWSING?

There are many paths, beliefs, and techniques which can help you attain ideal health, unlimited wealth, and the happiness you've always wanted. These techniques include Applied Kinesiology, muscle testing, meditation, channeling, yoga, Psych-K, tarot, and astrology, to name a few. Dowsing is also one of those paths. The technique of dowsing is so powerful, yet so simple everyone can learn to use it to enhance their life in every aspect. If you are open to dowsing, with a little practice, you can forever change your life and the lives of others.

Before you begin to dowse, it's important for you to understand that all things are composed of Energy or vibrating frequencies and that all things are connected because of the vibrating frequencies of Energy. This includes people, animals, business, thoughts, emotions, words, and situations. Even past and future events hold Energy. It's also important for you to understand that Energy never ceases to exist. This means that Energy never dies, and that the frequencies of Energy can be adjusted, changed, moved, and managed through the Power of our thoughts or intentions. Dowsing is simply learning how to tap into the sub-conscious and unconscious minds, where all answers and thoughts exist, and adjust the frequencies of vibrating Energy for our highest good.

For your own good, I want to stress the importance of always having good intentions when working with Energy in any form. Manipulating Energy through the use of any technique to destroy or harm someone's life is not in your own best interest. Do not go there!

History teaches us that dowsing isn't just some new age mumbo jumbo and that it isn't a hoax. In fact, it has been recorded throughout history that dowsing has been used in all areas of the world and for thousands of years. It has been used to locate objects, water, animals, and to find answers. Just as with its first historical recordings, dowsing continues to be one hundred percent accurate. If there is any inaccuracy in an answer or in finding something, it's important to *realize* that it is not the pendulum or the theory of dowsing that is flawed. The inaccuracy comes from asking incorrect questions or asking questions you are not ready to know the answers to. There is no question that dowsing is alive and well throughout the entire world and is still being widely used in mining, the oil and gas industries, and healing. It has and will continue to change the lives of millions of people.

Unfortunately, throughout history, the dowsing's reputation has been sullied by those who do not understand how it works or who have not learned to ask the right questions. If someone asks questions incorrectly at the wrong time, or for the wrong reasons, they will either receive wrong answers or no answers. When incorrect information is received and witnessed, people then claim that dowsing is a hoax and that it doesn't work. If you ask anyone who knows how and when to ask the right questions, they will guarantee that dowsing is one hundred percent accurate every time without exception and that it is no respecter of persons. It always works, always. This is why it's so important for you to learn how and when to ask the right questions. As you learn to ask correctly, you will begin to uncover layer after layer of yourself that in turn will allow you more insight to more questions that need to be asked. This will ultimately lead you to exactly what you need to know for your highest good. Don't let this sound complicated because it's not. You will find dowsing to be amazing and powerful work that is simple and enjoyable.

Other unfortunate perceptions have also been created throughout the years by people who use their dowsing abilities to show off their Power or to become famous. These people are not operating with good intentions and therefore will not have one hundred percent accuracy. They are the people who are responsible for causing others to regard dowsing and pendulum work as a hoax. They are wrong!

As your confidence and skill of dowsing increases you will often find that you already know what answer your pendulum is going to give you before it begins to move. With time and practice you may even find you know the answers before you ask them. Dowsing definitely increases your intuition and in time you may find that you don't need to use the pendulum as often as before to find your answers and healing. By learning to dowse, learning what questions to ask and when to ask them, you give yourself the opportunity to tap into unlimited resources and Power for every circumstance in your life. Sometimes it's easy to begin using a pendulum as a crutch, using it for every situation instead of listening first to your intuition. "Everything in moderation" is my policy. I suggest you make it yours as well. Once you begin dowsing, try to use your own intuition first when looking for an answer. Then if you don't have a clear answer, by all means pick up your pendulum and find your answers . . . because you've got them.

There will be only one reason why you wouldn't be able to learn to use this wonderful technique to help you through life and that is if you are unwilling. Be willing to learn and enjoy the benefits of saving time, money, frustration, heartache, and even embarrassment.

There are many instruments that can be used for dowsing. Witching sticks, divination rods, dowsing rods and pendulums are just a few of them. These are all just common physical materials but with time become uncommonly sensitive to your frequencies of Energy. There is no magic or Power in any pendulum or other instrument. Regardless of what you choose to work with, it serves only as a visual tool to show you that Energy is moving. Sometimes it's hard to have faith in something you can't see and that is why I believe dowsing is such a true gift. When you can see your pendulum respond, it helps to strengthen your faith or your belief. In addition to allowing you to see Energy moving, using a pendulum helps you focus your thoughts and intentions for an extended amount of time. When you clearly focus you have a greater possibility to connect to more information. This is why the practice of meditation is so powerful.

A pendulum simply reflects the patterns of vibrations or frequencies of the Energy you are working with. Your intentions, thoughts, and unlimited information, which are in your conscious, subconscious, and unconscious mind, all vibrate certain frequencies and those vibrations affect your nervous system which then affects your pendulum. Simply put, what's inside you is unlimited Power and that Power affects everything on every level, including your pendulum. This is why muscle testing is so effective. Your inner knowing affects your nervous system which affects your muscle strength. When the correct questions are asked and your muscles are tested, you will receive answers based on whether your muscle stays strong or whether it goes weak. Muscle testing is used extensively in diagnosing illnesses, injuries, Chiropractic alignment and in facilitating the changing of old beliefs and patterns. It's a wonderful technique that provides physical proof as does dowsing and is available to everyone for healing and answers.

If you're searching for answers to something you are highly emotional about, you may want to ask someone else to dowse for you. There have been occasions where I've seen deep desires and emotions affect the answer. Because the pendulum is so extremely sensitive to the vibrations of our thoughts and emotions, those thoughts and emotions can sometimes override the true answer. All I'm saying is be *aware* of your personal emotions when you dowse and be as open as you can about the outcome. With time and practice, you will learn to calm your emotions and desires and allow your Higher-Self to come through.

Pendulums can be made from a needle on thread, metal on string, crystals, or precious stones on chains. Almost anything can be used; there is no particular material that is better than another. I believe it is helpful, though, to choose a pendulum that you resonate with so you will enjoy looking at it and working with it. Once you choose your pendulum I suggest that you appreciate it, and use it only for your dowsing work. I generally don't let anyone else use my pendulum because it has a tendency to pick up some of their Energy. Not that this is a horrible thing, I just believe it can sometimes affect the accuracy. On several occasions I have allowed someone to use my pendulum while I'm teaching them to dowse. After our session, I set my intentions to clear it immediately and then at my next opportunity, clear it with sunshine and water and infuse it one hundred percent with my Energy again.

So find yourself a pendulum of whatever material you desire. Allow it to sit in the sun for a full day or if that isn't possible, run cold water over it for a few minutes as you set your intentions to clear it of all non-beneficial Energy. If it's possible, put your cleared pendulum under your pillow for one night and allow it to resonate with your frequencies as you sleep. This of course doesn't mean your pendulum won't work if you don't do this. By doing so, though, it increases your connection and infuses it for better response and accuracy. Set your intentions that your pendulum will always respond quickly and accurately for your highest good.

# CHAPTER 2

# GETTING STARTED

Learning to dowse with a pendulum is very simple. Learning the right questions to ask will take a little longer and will involve some time and practice. But the results will most certainly be worth it. If you have your pendulum, let's begin.

Place both feet on the floor, sit up straight and uncross your legs and feet. Close your eyes and take several slow steady breaths. Calm your thoughts. Allow yourself to be open and to know that you have the ability to learn this technique and that it will be a wonderful tool to use in your everyday life.

Hold your pendulum between your thumb and middle finger with your dominate hand. If it's more comfortable to hold it between your thumb and index finger, it's okay to hold it that way as well. When you first begin dowsing, try using your pendulum in both your right and left hand to find which hand gets the clearest response and feels the most comfortable. When you determine which hand works best, use that one. Rest assured, there is no right or wrong way to dowse except to cause harm to someone. This is all about what works for you.

Hold your pendulum lightly so your fingers do not become fatigued and let your other fingers extend outward. You may want to rest your elbow on your work surface until you are familiar with the movements of your pendulum. Once you become more accustomed to the feel of the different directions of your pendulum swinging, you will be able to dowse quickly and without the need for support. On occasion when my work goes on for any extended amount of time, my arm will begin to tire; I simply rest my elbow on my desk or support my forearm with my other hand and continue. You will find that some sessions are as short as five seconds while others may last as long as an hour. You always know it's time to stop when you get a clear stop from your pendulum or your thoughts begin to wander during the swinging of the pendulum.

Hold your pendulum somewhere out in front of you. My most comfortable position is with my arm anywhere between a 45 and 90 degree angle. You can ask your questions out loud or silently, it makes no difference. Now say **Please show me a yes answer**. Wait to see the direction of swing. In your mind think yes, yes, yes. In the beginning your pendulum may only move slightly and that's okay. You can ask for a clearer even stronger answer if you need to. When it stops, say **Please show me a no answer**. In your mind think no, no, no. When it stops say **Thank you**. Always, thank your Higher-Self or the Universe for the answers you receive. If at first you don't see any movement, be patient, take another calming breath and then ask again. You can do this. Stay open and positive and be tenacious.

If you begin to feel frustrated, put your pendulum down and come back to it later. I've seen people pick up their pendulum for the first time and immediately get clear answers while others have had to practice for months. It doesn't matter though. Just be open and allow yourself to believe. For most people, a yes answer is a forward and back swing and for others it may be a clockwise or counterclockwise swing. Once you have your established directions it will always be your unique answer and will never change . . . unless you want it to. You are the one in charge of establishing your communication system of dowsing. Remember that your pendulum reflects your intentions and vibrations and you are in charge.

In order for you to receive more in depth information and to successfully use the dowsing chart I've included, I suggest you set your intentions and the parameters for your pendulum to swing forward and back for yes and side to side for no. As you will see on the chart, a clockwise and counterclockwise swing is used for different answers.

If you look at the dowsing chart in the front of this book, you will see there are many directions the pendulum will swing depending on the answers and on the request being made. You can make your own chart if you choose or you can use the one I've created. If your intention is to use this chart, your pendulum will honor that intention and will swing according to the parameters that I have set. If you choose to make up your own chart, your pendulum will work according to it. It's whatever you want or intend and is all based on what works for you.

I have established my pendulum directions to be forward and back for yes, side to side for no, and no movement when I have asked an improper question that is not leading me to an answer I need to know at the time. My pendulum swings counterclockwise while I'm scrambling, cutting or removing frequencies and clockwise when transforming, surrounding, or placing new frequencies. The parameters of the included dowsing chart are based on what has worked for me.

You will experience much more accuracy while dowsing if you learn how to discipline and keep your thoughts focused on your question or phrase the entire time your pendulum is swinging. This will take practice as your mind will want to wander in the beginning. It's helpful to silently repeat your question over and over until your pendulum stops swinging. Some people like to close their eyes. I do not. I stay more focused when I keep my eyes on the pendulum the entire time. Remember that your pendulum is a conduit of Energy vibrations and that it is extremely sensitive to your vibrations, Higher Self, thoughts, or Universal Power. If your mind is wandering so might the accuracy of your pendulum. Over time, you will learn to discipline your thoughts. As you do, your accuracy will increase. Once the pendulum stops, always say **Thank you** either out loud or silently.

Most importantly, enjoy and have fun with your pendulum and be grateful every day for this gift that has shown up in your life.

Once you have established how to receive your answers with the direction of swing, you are ready to begin working with the Universal Energy that is inside you. You have the tools and the ability now to receive answers to anything . . . if it's to your highest good. It's all a matter of learning how, what and when to ask. And that's what we're going to do next.

# CHAPTER 3

# LEARNING HOW, WHAT, AND WHEN TO ASK

Let's begin by asking simple questions that you already know the answers to. For example, hold your pendulum in front of you and ask **Is my name Betty?** If your name is not Betty it will swing back and forth with a no answer. If your name happens to be Betty it will swing forward and back with a yes answer. Then ask **Is my name (say your real name).** Your pendulum will give you a yes answer. Make a statement saying **I have three children.** If you have three children it will swing yes. If you don't, it will swing no. Keep practicing with small questions or statements like these until you receive consistent movement and answers from your pendulum. As you get more comfortable, gradually begin to ask bigger questions. It is not necessary to ask your questions out loud unless you want to. All you need to do is simply *think* your question or statement.

In order to receive the most accurate answers you need to learn how to phrase your questions so they can be answered with a yes or no answer. With a little practice you will also be able to use the chart I have provided and begin to work with numbers and letters for more in depth answers. Be patient and thoughtful about your questions. You will not get a correct answer or any answer at all for that matter if you ask something like, **Which will my friends enjoy more for dinner tonight, Chicken Parmesan or Grilled Fish**? There is no way for your pendulum to respond unless you are using the chart, then it will more than likely swing to "Rephrase Question." The correct way to ask is **Will my guests enjoy Grilled Fish for dinner tonight**? This question allows for a yes or no answer. But you may want to ask if they would also enjoy Chicken Parmesan. You may get a yes answer to both questions. If you do, you can be confident that your dinner guests will enjoy whichever entrée you choose to serve. If you want to continue peeling layers for more precise information you could ask **Would my friends enjoy Chicken Parmesan more than Grilled Fish for dinner tonight**? Now you've reached a deeper layer where more information is available. You can rest assured that you will prepare the very entrée your guests will enjoy the most with the help of your pendulum. When you learn to ask the right questions, you can use your pendulum and this process to discern any kind of helpful information.

Here's another example of asking the right question. Not long ago someone asked me to dowse for them concerning several real estate properties they were considering as an investment. First I asked **May I work with this person**? Yes. Then I asked **Is it appropriate for me to dowse about this subject at this time**? Yes. If either answer would have been no, I would have politely told them it was not appropriate at this time for me to do the work. Even though I may not understand the answers I get, I ALWAYS respect the answer. ALWAYS! I then asked the person I was working with what it was she wanted to know or rather what her main question was. She was looking at several different pieces of real estate and wanted to know which piece of property would be the best investment and would give them the biggest return when it was sold. She was considering three different properties.

When you do this kind of work, it's important to take your time and form your questions so you can use the process of elimination. I took a couple calming breaths and thought for a few minutes. I began by writing each location on a piece of paper. I then pointed to each location one by one and asked **Will the purchase of this property be a good investment for Karla?** The answers were yes, yes, and no. One property was eliminated immediately. Now we had two to work with. I then pointed to both separately and asked **Will this property be a good investment for Karla?** Yes and yes. But I felt we needed to go deeper. So I asked **Which property will make Karla more money?** I pointed to the first one and got a no answer. Then I pointed to the second one and the answer was yes. There was her answer. Karla now knew which piece of property of the two would make her the most money. But again, I felt we needed to go even deeper with our questions. I wanted to make sure that this purchase was to her highest good and not just about the money. After all, making money on the property was just one question with one answer. There were a lot of other uncertainties and I wanted to make sure that she wouldn't have legal problems, water problems, or other unexpected issues that might come up throughout the purchase, ownership and resale. So I asked **Is the purchase of this property to Karla's highest good?** The answer was no! My pendulum said no! None of the three properties she was considering were to her highest good. We accepted the answer and said **Thank you.**

Because I have learned to trust the answers I get and I knew I had asked appropriate questions, I told her not to buy any one of the three properties. I then asked **Is there another property that Karla should**

13

consider at this time that will make her good money and will be to her highest good? Yes! She began looking for different properties immediately. When she located some new options, we dowsed again and found her the right property that would make her good money and would be a smooth transaction. She bought, fixed, sold, and made excellent money . . . without a hitch. By the way, she later found out that one of the other properties we had gotten a no answer on stayed on the market for a year. Asbestos had been found in the other one. Always trust!

Dowsing is such an amazing and wonderful tool. Anyone who has an open mind has the ability and the opportunity to learn how to use it. Be open and you will be able to tap into unlimited information. WARNING! Always use your pendulum for your highest good and for the highest good of others. It is not in your best interest to be vengeful, dishonest, or snoopy! Your subconscious mind knows what information you should and shouldn't know about and what you should and shouldn't ask. Your pendulum will certainly pick up on that Energy. Because your pendulum is a conductor of vibrations, your answers may not be accurate if you're asking inappropriate questions and in fact, you may not get any answers at all. Just be wise.

There have been times when I have asked a question and gotten a no answer even though I was sure it was going to be yes. If I'm ever confused or not comfortable with an answer, I have learned to leave it alone for the time being and come back to it later. Sometimes answers will remain constant, and sometimes they will change from hour to hour and even day to day. My first experience with a changing answer was a bit confusing. On this particular day, I asked my question and got a no answer. The next day I asked the same question and this time I got a yes answer. What I came to understand is that the first time I asked the question and got a no answer it was no at "that time." It was no for a reason. For what reason, I may never know and that's okay. My job is to trust and act on the answer I get "at the time." I never ask the same question twice in one session and I rarely ask the same question in the same day. I take the answer for what it is and move on. There are so many variables working at all times in our universe and our conscious mind is just not capable of knowing everything at once. On the other hand, our subconscious mind is capable and is *aware* of everything going on everywhere at all times. Dowsing enables us to tap into that information and that is why we need to learn to trust the answers and trust the timing. Trust your Higher Self. Trust the Universe.

Once in awhile I still get answers that are a bit confusing. When I do, I usually ask **Is it appropriate for me to ask this question at this time?** That lets me know if the time is appropriate. I have found that I usually get the confusing answers or changing answers when I have not asked this important question.

Do your best to not doubt your pendulum's accuracy. Learn that if you get a no answer, it does not always mean no will be the answer forever. It may just mean that no is the best answer "at this time." You will always, get the right answer at the time you ask if you ask the right questions. It could change within the hour but at "that time," you got the answer you needed to hear. Again, our conscious mind doesn't always know and understand everything that is going on around us at any given second so just trust! On the other hand, you may have phrased the question incorrectly and if you're using my dowsing chart, your pendulum will let you know that you need to rephrase your question.

I've listed below examples of what I've found to be very effective questions covering numerous subjects. I have also created a list of categories that I hope will be helpful to you while working on different subjects and events in your life and the lives of others with whom you may work. Some categories may repeat the same questions but there is a reason for it.

You will find that most of the questions and phrases I use are short. I find it's better to ask a lot of short questions rather than formulate long complicated ones. There's less confusion when you use short questions and it makes it easier to use the process of elimination.

You probably won't need to ask every one of these question every day, every week, or even every month. In time you will know exactly what you need to ask for yourself on a regular basis. Any time you're not sure what to ask, simply look at or point to each category one at a time, and as **Is there anything in this category I need to dowse over at this time for myself?** If it says yes to any particular one, stop and work your way through it before moving on. When you're finished with that category, come back to the list and continue asking if there are any more questions you need to ask in the remaining categories. Use the same process if you're working on behalf of another person.

When I begin a dowsing session for myself or for someone else, I always begin by asking **May I dowse for myself at this time?** If the answer is no, I do not continue. If the answer is yes, I move on to ask **May I dowse for _____ (the person I have in mind) at this time?** If the answer is no, I put my pendulum down . . . period. If the answer is yes, I proceed.

It's important to always begin a session by dowsing for yourself to make sure you are clear, open, and it's the appropriate time. If you get the go ahead and you are clear, move on. If you need adjusting in any area, ask for those adjustments to be made and then proceed.

Some of the following questions require only yes or no answers while others require use of the chart. This may seem time consuming in the beginning but your speed and your ability to know what to ask will increase with time and practice.

Ask **Am I switched?** If your pendulum says yes, you are *not* switched. If it says no, you *are*. If you are switched put your pendulum down, cross your hands and place your right index finger to the inside and below your left eyebrow and your left index finger to the inside and below your right eyebrow. Take in a deep breath and then exhale. Then uncross and switch which hand is in front and repeat the process. When finished, brush from your shoulder down to your finger tips with the opposite hand. Do this on both arms.

Now hold your pendulum close to your right shoulder just in front of your arm pit. It should begin swinging counterclockwise. Then move it in front of your left shoulder. It should change directions to swing clockwise. On occasion I've seen the pendulum swing the opposite directions. That is okay. This shows that your Energy is moving freely and you are ready to move on. If the pendulum does not switch directions, say **Please balance my Energy flow for my highest good.** Your pendulum will swing clockwise. After it stops, say **Thank you,** and move on.

Ask **Am I in balance with earth Energy?** If yes, move on. If no, say **Please adjust my frequencies to be in perfect balance with earth Energy.** Your pendulum will swing clockwise. When it stops, say **Thank you** and move on. Do not hesitate to ask this about your family, pets, home, school, and place of work.

Ask **Am I in balance with animal Energy?** This one is great because it allows you and animals of all kinds to have a spirit of comrade instead of fear and intimidation. Use the same principle as earth Energy. If yes, move on. If no, say **Please adjust my frequencies to be in perfect balance with animal Energy.** Your pendulum will swing clockwise.

Ask **Is my Energy level one hundred percent?** If you get a yes, move on. If you get a no, say **Please adjust my Energy level to its most appropriate place for my highest good.** Your pendulum will swing clockwise.

You can also use the chart for this question. By using the chart you will know exactly what your levels are, based on 100%. To use the chart, hold your pendulum in the center. Set your intention that your pendulum will swing to the 100 number to represent 100%. Then ask **Where is my Energy level at this time**? Your pendulum will swing to the exact number. If you're at 100%, move on. If you are not, let your pendulum continue swinging to and from the current number and say **Please adjust my Energy level to its most appropriate place for my highest good**. Allow the pendulum to do whatever it wants. For me, my pendulum swings back and forth at the number where I currently am, and gradually moves in the direction where I'm supposed to be. When it reaches 100%, it sometimes continues to swing from right to left for a few seconds before stopping and other times it stops almost immediately. When it stops, you are adjusted. You may need to adjust yourself everyday for months until your Energy is stable.

Remember that as you become more comfortable with dowsing your pendulum will begin to respond faster and faster to your questions. You will also find that you require less adjusting for yourself in many other areas.

Ask **Is my aura balanced**? If yes, move on. If no, say **Please balance my aura for my highest good**. Allow your pendulum to do what it wants. More than likely it will swing clockwise.

Ask **Are all my Chakras open and clear**? If yes, move on. If no, ask **May I clear and balance my Chakras at this time**? If no, go to the next subject. If yes, use the chart and begin with your 1st Chakra. Knowing where 100% is on the chart, ask **How open and free flowing is my 1st Chakra**? Your pendulum will swing to the exact number. Then say **Please open and clear my 1st Chakra for my highest good**. Some people like to say **Please open it to one hundred percent**. I like to let my Higher Self decide by saying **to my highest good**. What if one hundred percent isn't appropriate at the moment? Your Higher Self, the Universe knows exactly. Move on to each Chakra asking the same questions until all seven Chakras are open and clear. After you are more comfortable asking questions, you may want to learn what is causing your Chakras to become blocked. You will do this by asking questions about things that come to your mind. This is how you peel off more and more layers in order to heal yourself in any area.

Ask **Do I have any negative Energy affecting me at this time?** If no, move on. If yes, say **Please scramble the negative Energy that is adversely affecting me at this time.** Your pendulum will swing counterclockwise.

Ask **Do I have any negative entities in, on or around my Energy field? My body? My home? My work place?** If no, move on. If yes, say **Please remove any and all negative entities from my Energy field.** Then do this for your body, home and work place, if necessary. Your pendulum will swing counterclockwise. For more information about this subject, go to the section about "Negative Entities."

Ask **Do I have any non beneficial frequencies affecting me at this time?** If no, move on. If yes, say **Please scramble any and all non beneficial frequencies affecting me at this time.** Your pendulum will swing counterclockwise. Then say **Please transform these frequencies into something beneficial for my highest good.** Now your pendulum will swing clockwise.

Ask **Do I have any curses, hexes, vexes, spells, black magic, witchcraft, or bad medicine on me?** If no, move on, If yes in any of the areas; read more about them in the section titled "Curses."

Use the enclosed dowsing chart for the following questions. Knowing where 100% is located ask:

**What is my motivation level?** Your pendulum will swing to the current percentage. If it's not one hundred percent say **Please adjust my motivation level to its most appropriate place for my highest good.** Your pendulum will gradually swing to the 100% mark.

**What is my compatibility level?** If it's not one hundred percent say **Please adjust my compatibility level to its most appropriate place**

for my highest good. Your pendulum will gradually swing to the 100% mark. You can ask what your compatibility level is with any one you are wondering about. Simply ask **What is the compatibility level between me and _____ (other person, someone you work with, are thinking of dating, etc.)**? If it's not 100% and you want it to be, say **If it's to my highest good, please adjust the compatibility level between me and _____ (other person) to its most appropriate place for our highest good.**

What is my prosperity level? If it's not 100% say **Please adjust my prosperity level to its most appropriate place for my highest good.** Your pendulum will gradually swing toward the 100% mark.

**Am I operating with resistance on any level?** If yes, using 100% as the highest, ask **How much?** Say **Please remove any resistance I have concerning (whatever subject) for my highest good.** Your pendulum will swing counterclockwise.

For this next question you will first need to know your ideal body frequency. Ask **What is my ideal body frequency?** Your pendulum will let you know. Mine is 1 ½. Most people I have worked with are either 1 ½ or 2. When you know what yours is, say **Please adjust my body frequency to its most appropriate place for my highest good.** Your pendulum will swing back and forth moving gradually to its ideal place.

For more in depth work for either yourself or someone else, use the following questions to clear, balance, adjust, and gain needed knowledge. What you do with the knowledge is up to you. You can ask more specific questions, seek out natural healers and remedies, or you may feel more comfortable consulting western medicine. You are free to make your own choices concerning your emotions, health, and your spirituality.

More questions to ask:

Are there any demonic forces in my Energy field, body, home, or work?

Are there any negative Energy patterns present that need to be adjusted?

Am I compatible with my spirit guides?

How many spirit guides do I have? Use the chart for numbers or hold up fingers one at a time until you get a yes. You even have the ability to learn their names if you choose by using the letters on the chart.

Do I have any psychic cords that need to be cut at this time?

Do I have any old contracts, vows, or agreements that need to be ended?

Do I have any old beliefs that need to be changed? (This one will have many, many layers!)

Do I have any fungus in my body that needs to be addressed?

Are there any viruses in my body?

Are there any non-beneficial bacteria in my body?

Are there any parasites in my body?

Is there any cancer present in or on my body?

Are there any tumors in or on my body?

Do I have any allergies I need to be aware of at this time?

(Use the process of elimination by asking questions about foods and environment that can be answered with a yes or no.)

Am I allergic _____?

Do I need to be taking any vitamin supplements at this time?

What supplements are to my highest good? Ask by name and brand.

How much should I take? Use the chart for numbers or hold up fingers one at a time until you get a yes.

*Using 100% on the chart ask the following questions:

What is my brain chemistry balance?

What is my body chemistry balance?

What is my red blood cell level?

What is my white blood cell level?

What is my serotonin level?

What is my melatonin level?

What is my body pH level?

What is the truth level of this book (or any other book)?

What is the truth level of _____ (something you've heard, read, believed, or even a religion)?

What is the honesty level of _____ (a particular person)?

What is the level of integrity of _____ (anything you want to know about)?

*The following questions will bring yes or no answers:

Is _____ (person) honest?

Can I trust _____ (person)?

Am I being affected by any harmful:

Subliminal messages

Frequencies

Pollutants caused by:

Power lines

Chemical plants

Water

Anything buried in the ground

Television

Music

Computer games

Video games

If yes to any of the above questions, go through each one and say: **Please scramble and adjust the frequencies that are causing (me or a**

I want to share another example of what happened with a friend of mine who was on her way to Denver to buy a car. She was having a hard time deciding between two different styles of vehicle and wondered which one she would enjoy the most and which one would best meet her needs. While she was driving to Denver, she called and asked if I could help her with her decision. I quickly asked which car would be to her highest good. We got her answer and she drove it home. It's that simple and that handy. Dowsing can save you time, money, frustration, and even pain.

As you can see, you have the ability to ask just about anything including when a person's birthday is, what year they were born, what is the best book for you to read at this time, even what direction you are facing if you're lost somewhere. There are unlimited questions you can ask to improve, empower, and heal your life and the life of others. Be creative, have fun, and keep it simple.

# CHAPTER 4

# A DEEPER LEVEL

The following categories are a few of the unlimited questions that encompass your entire existence physically, emotionally, socially, financially, and spiritually. All you need to do is keep an open mind and continue learning how to form questions that can be answered using your pendulum. I trust these questions will provide a starting place for you in your search for healing and answers. With each layer of information you peel off, you will be able to move on and form your own questions as more and more layers unfold. Trust that you will be led to what you need to know at the right time.

# Energy Work

This is one of my most used practices of dowsing. It's done by simply asking for the most appropriate Energy to be placed around people, animals, and events. Once dowsing becomes a part of your life you will find yourself looking at things in a much more positive way and that your intentions are always going in the direction of what's to the highest good for not only yourself but all of mankind. I know you will find it very rewarding and fulfilling.

All you need to do is say **Please place the most appropriate Energy around** _____ **(person, place, or event) for** _____ **(whatever outcome it is you want) for their highest good.** Your pendulum will swing clockwise. **Thank you.**

## *Example:*

Someone I was dowsing for was quite nervous about a very important job interview. I asked **Is this particular job would be to her highest good?** The answer was yes. I then asked to **Please place the most appropriate Energy around Laurie, around each person that will be interviewing her and around the office they will be meeting in, so she will be calm, able to answer questions intelligently and articulately, and that each person interviewing her will be impressed and will offer her the position of her dreams and will pay her well.** It went perfectly. She was offered more than she expected and she loves her job.

Do this for anyone or any event such as entertaining, holidays, vacations, shopping, meetings, doctors' visits, attorneys, accountants, fitness centers, workouts, hair salons, business meetings, and performances. Use your imagination and have fun.

# Aura Balancing

An aura is a colorful Energy field that surrounds everything that is alive. It is visible to some people and invisible to others. The movement and colors of the Energy or aura of a person represents what they are experiencing physically, emotionally, and spiritually. There are many reasons why an aura can become unbalanced. Through dowsing you have the ability to ask what is going on and what needs to be done. If your aura is ever out of balance it's very easy to correct. Hold your pendulum and say **Please balance my aura (or the aura of other people) for my (or his/her) highest good.** Allow your pendulum to swing clockwise for as long as needed. Then say **Thank you.** That's it. If you want to go a level deeper and find out why your aura is out of balance, you will need to ask more questions and use the process of elimination.

# Chakra Clearing and Balancing

Chakras are Energy centers located throughout the body. The seven main chakras are aligned in an ascending column from the base of the spine to the top of the head. Each Chakra is believed to represent and resonate with specific aspects of consciousness, emotions, colors, animals, earth elements, and a musical key.

1st Chakra—Located at the base of the spine resonates with the color red, the earth, survival and grounding.
2nd Chakra—Located in the lower abdomen resonates with the color orange, water, emotions, sexuality, and desire.
3rd Chakra—Located in the solar plexus resonates with the color yellow, will, Power, anger, and joy.
4th Chakra—Located in the heart area resonates with the color green, air, love, balance, and compassion.

5th Chakra—Located in the throat area resonates with the color blue, communication, creativity, and excitement.

6th Chakra—(third eye) Located in the forehead resonates with the color indigo, clairvoyance, psychic abilities, imagination, and dreaming.

7th Chakra—Located at the crown of the head resonates with the color violet, thoughts, one's spiritual connection, understanding, knowing, bliss, and the Higher Self or God.

Each Chakra carries vibrational energies corresponding to our emotions, actions, health, or spirituality. Using your pendulum you can determine if any one of your Chakras are blocked or is under or overactive.

This is a two-part question and you begin by asking **Do any of my Chakras need clearing at this time?** And then **Do any of my Chakras need balancing at this time?** If you get a no, move on. If you get a yes, do the following.

Put your attention on your 1st Chakra and ask: **Does my 1st Chakra need clearing at this time?** If no, ask: **Does my 1st Chakra need balancing at this time?** If no, move on to the 2nd Chakra and continue through your 7th Chakra, clearing and balancing each one that needs to be done.

If you get a yes on a Chakra needing clearing say: **Please clear any blocks in my 1st (or whatever number) Chakra at this time for my highest good.** Your pendulum will swing counterclockwise. When it stops, say **Please balance my 1st Chakra at this time for my highest good.** Your pendulum will swing clockwise. Do this for each Chakra that needs to be cleared and balanced. Say **Thank you.** If you want to go a level deeper and find out why your Chakras are blocked, you will need to ask more questions and use the process of elimination.

## Negative Entities

Negative entities are forms of Energy vibrations. I liken them to bad vibes. They can be picked up from people who greatly dislike, despise or are jealous of you; from extremely negative and hateful situations; or from negative movies, books, and music. Negative entities can sometimes be harmful if not cleared and can often cause a variety of illnesses, diseases, emotional problems, addictive and abusive behaviors, and even suicide. They can sometimes be similar to what some people think of as a demonic possession.

There is no need to be afraid of negative entities though, as the frequencies are easy to scramble by using your intentions and dowsing over them. It most definitely does not take a Catholic Priest or people praying in tongues or laying on of hands to remove them, even though I've seen that work. You even have the ability to do this work easily from a distance for someone else. Remember, Energy knows no time or distance. It is here and it is now. Always! This is why you can dowse and remove old frequencies from past events, people who have passed over and even situations in other lifetimes.

Begin by asking **Do I (or the person you're working with) have any negative entities in my Energy field or body?** If yes, ask **May I remove these entities at this time?** If no, go to another subject. If yes, ask **Is it important for me to know how many there are?** If no, move on. If yes, use the chart and hold your pendulum in the center while you ask **How many entities are in my Energy field or body?** Your pendulum will swing to the correct number.

If you like you can ask **Is it important for me to know the strength of these entities?** If no, move on. If yes, use the chart to determine the strength of each entity as it is sometimes important to understand how much an entity is affecting you or another person. Ask **Of 100% how much is this entity (or these entities) affecting my life?** If you get this far, you may want to ask **Is it important for me to know where**

**it came from**? I always ask this question. I believe it's important for you or the person you are working with to gain an *awareness* of where negative entities exist, what it is you may exposing yourself to, and to become *aware* of what is causing them to attach to you. When you know where they're coming from it's easier to protect yourself by either staying away, or placing a shield of protection around you.

Now that you have gathered this information, it's time to scramble and remove the negative entity.

Holding your pendulum say **Please scramble and remove the frequencies and life force of any and all negative entities that are in my Energy field or body so that they may never harm me again**. Your pendulum will swing counterclockwise.

Then say **Please place a shield of protection around me so they may never harm me again**. Your pendulum will swing clockwise. Say **Thank you**.

If you know you are going to be around negative entities or you begin to feel them, whether you have your pendulum available or not, in your mind, say **Please place a shield of protection around me to protect me from any negative entities or harmful Energy**. You will be protected.

If the negative entities show a great deal of influence in your life, they may need to be dowsed over more than once. You'll know when you are clear of them by asking. If you don't have the result you want, you may need to see if you are operating under any resistance. I have found that some people actually like the symptoms of negative entities such as overeating, or overindulging and therefore don't want to completely let go of the affect of the negative entity. This is often the case with smokers, alcoholics, porn addicts, and/or other unhealthy addictions. If you think this may be the case, ask **Do I have any resistance to letting go of this negative entity**? If no, continue the normal scrambling on a regular basis until you are clear. If yes, say **Please remove all** resistance I am experiencing in letting go of this negative entity. Your pendulum will swing counterclockwise. Then you can ask to scramble the frequencies of the entity again.

A particular person I worked with had a negative entity that was affecting 80% of her life. That's quite a bit. She was experiencing overeating, excessive drinking, and binge shopping. She asked me to dowse over her because she wanted to stop her actions but couldn't seem to. I began asking questions to find out what was causing her behavior and I found that it was one negative entity. I asked the strength of the entity; it was 80%. Then I asked if it was important that we knew where it came from. Yes, it was important. By asking layered questions, I learned that she had been in a weakened state; tired, stressed from work, kids, etc., and had been listening to a particular music CD. I asked if there were negative entities imbedded in that CD. Yes! I asked if that's where it came from. Yes! Now we knew what we were working with.

I first asked to remove her resistance and then to remove and destroy the negative entity. In a very short time, she lost ten pounds and put herself on a budget! Awesome! Oh, by the way, she broke the CD and threw it away.

You can use this technique on yourself, people, animals, and property. Just have no fear and go for it!

## Psychic Cords

Psychic cords are very interesting strands of Energy. Most people aren't even *aware* of them. They are simply projections of Energy that stay attached between people and/or events until they are cut either intentionally or sub-consciously. Psychic cords can mildly or dramatically affect people in many different ways. They can influence beliefs, thoughts, emotions, actions, relationships, situations, events, and most definitely, your health and body.

I have found both beneficial and non-beneficial cords. The beneficial ones are a mute point. Just be grateful for them. If you're curious, you can ask to find out who they are coming from and where they are attached.

The non-beneficial ones have three categories:

Going from you to another person or event
Coming from another person or event to you
Attached in both directions

What you want to do is cut any and all non-beneficial cords in all directions. This can be done easily. I've done this for a lot of people and have witnessed everything from emotional releases such as crying, laughter and joy, to a physical feeling like a rush or jolt. Others felt a temporary weakness from the release. Others didn't feel much of anything physically or emotionally, but they did experience a shift in events soon after the dowsing session.

Begin by asking **Do I have any non-beneficial psychic cords coming from me at this time?** If yes, and you're curious, you can ask **How many?** I find it beneficial to know where they are coming from on you and where they are attached to on the other person and vice versa. In every case I've dowsed to cut psychic cords, they have been attached to one, several or all of the seven Chakras. Knowing this will help you understand what you and the other person may be experiencing in your lives. As you know, each Chakra represents areas of your life and these cords directly affect the Energy flow of the Chakra to which it's attached.

First, find out with what person or event you are dealing with. Ask **Are they attached to _____ (begin asking names until you find who it is)?** Then ask **Are they coming from my 1st Chakra?** If no, move through all seven to get your answers. You may only have them coming from one Chakra, or three or all seven. Then ask **Are they** attached to _____ (the other person's) 1ˢᵗ Chakra? Then move through all seven for your answer, if you want to know. This step isn't necessary, but, again, I find it helpful in peeling off layers for deeper understanding and healing, especially in relationships.

Before moving forward, you need to stop and ask **Is it to my highest good to cut these cords at this time?** ALWAYS ASK THIS QUESTION. Sometimes those cords need to stay in place for awhile or until you've completed your contract with that person. Your Higher Self knows what you need, so ask.

If you get a clear go ahead, cut the cords. Say **Please cut any and all non-beneficial psychic cords coming from me (or my number Chakra) that are attached to _____ (the other person and their number Chakra). Please scramble their frequencies so they may never re-attach or cause me any pain or harm again.** Your pendulum will swing counterclockwise.

It is quite common to have cords coming from several Chakras. I suggest that you do this for each individual Chakra. Allow your pendulum to stop before moving on to the next number. Work your way from your 1ˢᵗ Chakra upward. I find it beneficial to visualize a white light, or sharp knife, even scissors cutting the cords from close to your body. See the cord snap back to the other person or event and the space between you begin to clear. This is powerful work so take your time and breathe deeply. When you finish, be extremely grateful! This is huge.

Now we begin our work in the other direction by asking **Are there any non-beneficial psychic cords coming from _____ (the other person) that are attached to me?** If no, your work is finished. Say **Thank you.** If yes, ask **Are they attached to my 1ˢᵗ Chakra?** And begin to work your way upward through number seven. It isn't necessary, but if you want to know where they are coming from on the other person, you may ask. Once you've established how and at what location that person is connected to you, ask **Is it to my highest good to cut** these cords at this time? If no, your work is finished for now. No, does not mean no forever, just at this time. The cords may need to be cut tomorrow, next week or even next month. If yes, say **Please cut any and all non-beneficial psychic cords coming from** _____ **(their name) that are attached to my (number) Chakra (or me). Please scramble their frequencies so they may never re-attach or cause any pain or harm again.** Your pendulum will swing counterclockwise. Again, let your pendulum stop before moving on to the next Chakra. When you have finished, be grateful because you are now free!

I was once working with someone who was going through a divorce. Both parties were having a very difficult time. During my work, I asked about psychic cords and if they were part of the cause of so much turmoil. Yes, yes, and yes! It was so amazing. When I finished my work in cutting cords in both directions, things settled down almost immediately. Never doubt that you are moving a lot of Energy and doing a lot of healing work with your focused intentions. Always, always ask permission and do your work for the highest good of yourself and others. Always!

## Curses

If you have dowsed to find you are dealing with curses, hexes, vexes, spells, witchcraft, or bad medicine, here is what I have found to be effective.

If you have a yes answer to any one of the above, ask **May I remove this curse (hex, vex, spell, witchcraft, or bad medicine) at this time?** If no, don't. If yes, ask **Is it important that I know where this curse (etc.) came from?** If no, move on. If yes, start asking your questions. Here's something you need to know.

Curses or spells are nothing more than being totally convinced of the belief you're operating under. The good news is that you are in charge of your beliefs and you can change them any time you are willing. You are under the influence of a curse or hex, if you are totally convinced of whatever another person is telling you. What I find most common is that people pick up curses from someone who has obsessive negative thoughts or hateful, even dangerous, thoughts about them. Fear of that person shifts your Energy thus allowing you to fall under curses, hexes, vexes, spells, witchcraft, or what some call bad medicine. The first thing to do is to end the fear immediately. You must *realize* that you are in charge of your thoughts, your beliefs, and your behaviors. You . . . no one else. It's time to take back your Power by changing what you believe and removing the curse.

My personal experience with a curse was brought to my conscious mind through dowsing. I found that I had been operating under a curse since I was eight years old. The full story of this is in my book *Changing the Face of God*. What I uncovered using my pendulum is that I completely believed what one of my religious grade school teachers had told me when I was eight years old. This teacher used to make me and my classmates spend hours a day memorizing chapters from the King James Bible. We would have to stand in front of the whole school before the day was over and recite not just one, but several chapters with no mistakes. If we failed, she would smack us with a ruler, ridicule us right there in front of everyone, and tell us that if we were better children we would be able to "remember" what we were supposed to, that God was very disappointed in us and she hoped that we would make it to heaven. Then for our punishment, we were given additional chapters to memorize by the next day. As I mentioned, I was only eight years old at the time and had no *awareness* of how deep my fear was of her, of losing my salvation, and of God, all because I couldn't "remember" 200 versus from the Bible. So there I was one day in front of the whole school. It was my turn to perform. After I had recited somewhere around the 148th verse from memory, my mind went absolutely blank. I couldn't remember a thing. I couldn't even remember what I had just recited. It was gone. Well, I was told how stupid I was, that I couldn't learn anything, that I had surely disappointed God, and I would never be able to remember anything. What do you think my new belief was? I was going to hell for making mistakes, I was stupid and I couldn't remember anything. Through fear and humiliation, this teacher completely manipulated my mind. She made me feel inadequate by putting me down, by chipping away at my self-esteem, and by humiliating me in front of the rest of my class. I was totally convinced; I believed everything she had told me. I had lost my own personal belief in myself, my Power, by taking on her beliefs. My belief that I could learn had been overridden with her belief that I was stupid. My vibrational frequencies had been lowered to hers and would resonate with hers for the next forty years whether she knew it or not. It was a curse.

In order for me to get free I had to first become aware of the disempowering belief I was operating under, remove the Energy from it, form new beliefs, and affirm them.

When you empty yourself of your personal beliefs and take on the belief of someone else, you are actually giving that other person your Power. When you have no self esteem or personal beliefs, you are always looking for esteem from someone or something else "outside" of yourself. Without self-esteem or belief in yourself, you are powerless to believe anything different from what the person in authority over you is telling you. It's called mind control. And if you believe the other person totally, that belief becomes a curse or a spell. But any belief can be changed! When someone has that much mind control over you, you are under their spell, and you will stay under their spell or curse or mind control until you have the *awareness* and resources to break it.

Breaking it is accomplished by changing the belief to what you want it to be, a belief that empowers you. You're tapping into the resources that can help you do that right now! You can now take back your self-esteem, your Power, your beliefs, and break any curse you need to. It doesn't matter if the person whose curse you've been under is alive or dead, you are still under their spell, living their belief until you free yourself. Rest assured, you can free yourself or another person from any curse, spell, or mind control any time you're ready to by setting your intentions, dowsing and asking the right questions.

It took me almost forty years to gain the *awareness* that I was under a curse, where the curse came from, and that I had the ability to change the belief and the harmful effects this woman had had on me. The way she manipulated my mind affected me on a very deep level, in fact so deep the memories of that experience were embedded right in my cells. It's what is called cellular memory. This is when our cells are embedded with and carry emotional memories, good and bad until we clear them. Cellular memory will eventually manifest physically either in a good way which is vibrant health or in a bad way which is sickness and disease. This is the very reason why it's so important to clear yourself of negative emotions and curses before they manifest in the form of sickness, disease, or accidents. You may have heard examples of how cellular memory comes to the surface of people's bodies in the form of bruises, hand prints or whip marks, when people go under hypnosis or during a powerful Energy clearing process. I've witnessed this phenomenon and it is most certainly and undeniably powerful to watch a person's old beliefs physically come to the surface and then be cleared away. Have No Fear! This is life empowering work and it's all available right now.

Let's continue. I'm assuming that you are now *aware* of the curse or belief that you or someone else has been operating under and you may or may not know where it came from. Before we begin ask **Is it to my highest good to remove this curse at this time?** If no, stop and come back to this at a later time. If yes, it is helpful to know what the belief is and change that belief as you've learned how to do previously. If you aren't *aware* of the belief move on anyway and say **Please remove and neutralize any and all curses on me (or the other person or property) at this time**. Your pendulum will swing counterclockwise. Now say **Please place a shield of protection around me from ever taking on those beliefs again**. Your pendulum will swing clockwise. Do not forget to say **Thank you** when it stops.

If you feel you need deeper work, turn to the "Beliefs" section and go through the steps. Remember, curses are a reflection that you are totally convinced of a harmful and disempowering belief. If you can identify the belief that needs to change, you can change it.

## Past Life Issues

There is the possibility that old past life issues, beliefs, thoughts, intentions, and/or imprints can be carried forward into this life. You can find out if this is the case by simply asking **Do I have any unresolved past life issues that need to be cleared at this time**? If no, you're work is finished on this subject at this time. If you answer is yes, ask **Is it important that I know exactly what this concerns**? If no, move on. If yes, you will need to ask questions to find out when, where, and what needs to be cleared. You'll want to ask if you have any attachment to happenings such as:

| | |
|---|---|
| Rejection | Betrayal |
| Abuse | Inquisition |
| Persecution | Abduction |
| Humiliation | Rape |
| Unrequited love | Frustration |
| Stress of any kind | Suffering |
| Drowning | Burning |
| Hanging | Crucifixion |
| Stabbing | Beheading |

| | |
|---|---|
| Poisoning | Stoning |
| Gunshot | Natural disaster |
| Disease | War |
| Suffocating | Torture |
| Starvation | Incest |

Or anything else you may think of.

You can also find out the percentage of how much of your past is affecting your life or particular situation at this time. I find it helpful to do this step as I can watch the percentage of the effect lower with each dowsing session. When you are ready to clear, say **Is it to my highest good to clear these unresolved past life issues at this time?** If no, you're work is finished at this time. If yes, say **Please scramble and remove the life force from any beliefs, thoughts, emotions, or imprints, I may have in this body on all levels, on all levels of my consciousness and in all directions of time.** Your pendulum will swing counterclockwise. When it stops say **Please transform this Energy into the most appropriate Energy for my highest good.** Your pendulum will swing clockwise. Say **Thank you!**

You can immediately ask what the percentage of effect is. It should be lower. It may take several sessions to clear the old Energy. Always ask if the time is appropriate.

## Ghosts

Working with ghosts does not have to be threatening or scary as portrayed by Hollywood. It is as simple as working with negative entities. Be confident and be in charge.

A ghost is a left-over fragment of Energy that was once a living person. Occasionally, at the time of the person's death, some of their Energy or Life Force gets left behind. This left behind Energy is simply a fragment of their being. Fragments that are left behind can be small and cause memories or feelings, while large fragments can appear to be the actual person hovering, moving or walking and can sometimes cause things to move around. A fragment of left behind Energy is unconscious information or vibrations that remain from the former life and continues looping on its self. It does not think, it just vibrates and loops. This can go on forever. Understand that Energy does not have a conscious mind. It's the human body that has the conscious mind. You may have heard stories of people who begin seeing their loved ones or feeling them for several days or weeks after they have passed over. Often they will see a form of their loved one standing at the foot of their bed in the night or sometimes objects will be moved in their house. After several days or even weeks, the fragments gradually fade and they are never seen again. This is because this fragment of Energy gradually absorbs into the collective Energy field and dissipates. It's a little bit like memories fading from your mind. Most fragments fade with time as well.

On other occasions, these fragments are larger and seem to be stuck or unable to absorb into the Universal Energy field for some reason. These left over fragments or "ghosts" are vibrating frequencies of unconscious memories and/or intentions of the deceased person. The vibrations of these memories and intentions are what can be felt or seen by those still living. What causes fragments to be left behind? The same thing that causes us to have memories about someone or some event. Vibrational frequencies. These frequencies or "ghosts" that are affecting you or someone you know are usually stuck here because of the emotional state of the person at the time of their death.

Fragments being left behind usually have to do with the way the person died or what they were thinking at the time of their death. These vibrating emotional memories sometimes have a message for someone because that's what the person had wanted to do right when they died but didn't get the chance. It's this leftover vibration or frequency of the intention the person had at the time of their death that gets stuck. Once the message gets across or is delivered to the living person through various means, the fragment will almost always dissipate. Other fragments of deceased people are just plain ornery or stubborn and are left behind because that was the intention of the person when he died. The deceased was stubborn and ornery, and his intent was to pester people from now on. There are also fragments or "ghosts" that have no intentions. They can't move on because someone living won't let go.

I'm sure you've read many stories about ghosts haunting houses or buildings or pestering someone. These fragments or "ghosts" usually stem from the intentions of the person who passed over and need to get a message to someone so they can dissipate and move on. Dowsing can help do just that.

First begin by asking **Is it appropriate for me to do this work at this time?** If yes, say **Please place a shield of protection around me and this entire area.**

Now ask **Is this the ghost of a deceased person needing to move on?** If no, I would begin to ask if you're working with negative Energy or negative entities. See those categories if that's what you're working with and don't forget to ask for permission. If it is a ghost, ask **May I help this ghost over to the other side?** If the answer is no, leave it alone and say **Please place the most appropriate Energy around this place for the highest good of everyone who enters.** Your job is finished. But if you get the go ahead say **Is there a message this ghosts needs to get across to someone?** If yes, use the alphabet on the chart to get the message. You will need to ask your pendulum to swing to each letter to write what needs to be said and who needs to hear it. Say **Please write the message for me at this time.** Then **Who needs to hear this message?** You will want to ask **May I share this message** with this person at this time? When you get that answer, ask if the ghost needs to cross to the other side now? If no, you're finished except to share the message. If yes, say **I ask now that this ghost be released to cross over to the other side where it may continue its journey in peace.** Your pendulum will swing clockwise.

If there is no message, ask **Is this ghost stuck and in need of crossing over?** If no, you're finished. If yes, say **Is there someone keeping this ghost here that needs to let it go?** If no, move on. If yes ask **May I release this ghost from the living person so it may move on?** If no, move on. If yes, say **Please cut any non-beneficial energetic cords between this ghost and the living person that is keeping this Energy stuck.** Your pendulum will swing counterclockwise. When it stops say **I ask now that this ghost be released to cross over to the other side where it may continue its journey in peace.** You are finished. Consequently, the person who was attached will be released as well.

If these are not the situations, ask **Is this ghost ornery and wanting to taunt people but needs to cross over?** If no, you're finished. If yes, say **I ask now that this ghost be released to cross over to the other side where it may continue its journey in peace.**

When you have completed your dowsing say **Please place the most appropriate Energy around this place and these people (who either live there or were being bothered) for their protection and for their highest good.**

Be grateful for the ability you have to do this type of work.

## Life Force and Energy Levels

One of the things you will find extremely helpful is to always have your Energy level and life force at 100%. Simply say **Please raise my Energy level (or life force) to its most appropriate place for my highest good.** Your pendulum will swing clockwise.

If you find yourself continually needing to adjust your levels, there is almost always a reason for it being low and it is to your highest good to find out why. So, instead of asking everyday to raise the Energy level, I suggest you find out what's bringing it down and deal with the cause. Begin by asking questions about negative energies, psychic cords, or disempowering beliefs until you find the source of what's lowering your Energy level and/or life force. When you find the source and remove it or transform it, your Energy level and life force won't need adjusting so often. Almost every time I've gone to the source, cleared it, and then come back to check the Energy level, the level has already adjusted to 100% without my asking. What this tells me is that you can continue to adjust your levels daily but the low Energy level or life force is only a symptom of a deeper problem that can easily be cleared. It's a lot like taking a prescription drug. The drug is making you feel better the way raising your Energy level for the day makes you feel better, but they're both masking the problem. Find the root of the problem, deal with it, and then you won't need the drug or in the case of Energy levels, you won't need to continually adjust it. Just for your information, it's rare that your life force or that of someone else will need adjusting more than once or twice in a year unless there is a disease or some deep belief or emotion that needs attention. Energy levels are affected more easily and will need more attention and adjusting.

Know that everything has an Energy level and a life force so don't hesitate to ask to adjust your home, business, people, and events, past, present, and future. Your abilities and opportunities are unlimited.

## Frequencies

Most people's ideal body frequency is somewhere between 1 and 2. Mine is 1 ½ and is the same for most of the people I have worked with. Yours may be different. Simply ask and use the chart so you'll know.

Once I was commissioned to work with someone whom I disliked greatly. Even though I truly didn't want to do the work, I kept getting the go ahead from my pendulum (my higher self). I knew what I was supposed to do and I knew that it would be to their highest good and mine as well if I did the work. So I moved forward. For some time I had allowed this person to cause a great deal of stress and pain in my life but when I began to change and heal myself, I was led to help and heal her as well and without her ever knowing about it. I believe this is what the great teacher Jesus was talking about when he said to pray for your enemies. It isn't the easiest thing I've ever done, but I will say it was one of the more rewarding. Of course there is only so much you can do for another person because he or she is resistant, but every little bit of Energy work you do, will cause change to occur, mostly in yourself but also in the life of the other person.

In this case, I began by asking what her ideal body frequency should be. It was 1 ½. I asked what it was currently. It was 47! Now you don't have to be a brain surgeon to know that the difference of those numbers means something is terribly wrong. This person had plenty wrong in her life. Without giving details, I will just tell you that over a period of months, their body frequency lowered to 28 and there was a major shift in the role this person played in my life as well as I in theirs. Currently as I write, her frequency is still 28, but it's definitely better. I truly hope her life will be happy one day. In the mean time, dowsing has allowed me to be free from her negativity.

This story of adjusting frequencies happens to be one extremely close to my heart.

One morning one of my very best friends called me to say she was on her way to the doctors because she had just found a lump on the neck of her thirteen-year-old son. She asked me to dowse and call her back. I did my normal dowsing for myself and then asked for permission to dowse about this situation. I got the go ahead and began my questions. I'm going to say right now, be very *aware* and cautious of what you're asking. You want to make sure you can handle the answers and that you will trust and do what you are asked to do. This work is not to be taken lightly. There is a huge amount of responsibility that goes along with learning to dowse.

After many layers of questions, I got an answer about my friend's son. I asked if it was to her highest good to know the answer. Yes.

That phone call was one of the hardest calls I've ever had to make. It was cancer. I began by telling her "you need to be prepared for what the doctor is going to tell you. What he says may not be as it seems . . . and that everything was in order." That's what came out of my mouth and I wasn't sure what it all meant until later.

The blood tests came back to the first attending doctor; he said that he thought it was underactive thyroid. They felt relieved, but I knew better deep down; so did my friend. Two days later another doctor read the tests. He immediately called her and her husband and said "pack your bags because you're on your way to Denver Children's Hospital. Your son has stage four cancer." Now we understood what "things may not be as they seem" meant. I also understood that she needed a couple of days to prepare for what the doctor was going to tell them. Because of the dowsing and the information she received, she had those two days to prepare herself on a deep level so that when her family got the news, she could be strong for them. It happened just as it should have. Everything was in order.

As things progressed, I was asked to stay very involved. My knowledge of dowsing helped support the family in medical diagnoses, treatments, and other difficult decisions. I knew from the beginning that there was some energetic work that needed to be done and that I would do it if I were asked.

I believe that all disease, including cancer, has an Energy frequency and that any frequency can be scrambled and transformed. There are many highly effective ways to scramble frequencies and dowsing is only one of them. You must know what questions to ask, though!

I didn't have a go ahead on dowsing for him until his third day of his first round of chemo. I began my dowsing session for my girlfriend's son by arranging my questions in an order of what needed to be done for his highest good. I started out by asking permission. Yes! Next I got all his ideal frequencies and levels and wrote them down. Then I asked where he was currently in each area and wrote them down. I then asked in what order I needed to work to clear, scramble, destroy, and transform. Now I had my plan of action.

His ideal body frequency was 1 ½. It was currently 44.
His ideal life force was of course 100%. It was currently 70%.
His ideal Energy level was 100%. It was currently 14%.
His ideal immune system was 100%. It was currently 9%.
The cancer's frequency was 60.
His pain level was 20%.
His aura needed to be balanced.
His 1st, 2nd, and 3rd Chakra needed clearing and balancing.
He had several beliefs that needed to be cleared.

My instructions were to begin by scrambling the frequency of the cancer in his body. When I asked, my pendulum almost swung out of my hand. It was flying around so hard it was actually catching on my thumb. I just kept saying my request over and over in my head until it stopped. It took quite awhile. I then asked what his body frequency was now. It immediately lowered from 44 to 36. There was more work to be done and I continued by asking to lower his pain level to zero. I checked his body frequency again and it was now down to 29. His body frequency was getting better without my asking because I was working on the *cause* not the symptom. Out of curiosity, I asked what the cancer frequency was now . . . ZERO. Nice. I then asked to raise his immune system to 100% so that he would not contract any illnesses or other diseases. Again my pendulum flew around and around and this time continued for an even longer time. That lowered his body frequency to 25. Every time there was a transformation in Energy, his frequency got better. The Chakras were next. His 1st Chakra was 100% blocked, his 2nd 30% blocked, and his 3rd 70% blocked. I asked for each Chakra to be cleared then balanced. As my pendulum swung I could see the colors of his Chakras begin to flow again. It was like the colors of the rainbow and totally amazing. His body frequency was now 12! Finally I asked for his aura to be balanced.

After each area was addressed I rechecked all the numbers.
His body frequency was 1 ½ from 44.
His life force was 100% from 70%.
His Energy level was 100% from 14%.
His immune system was 100% from 9%.
The cancer was 0 from 60.
His pain was 0 from 20%.

During that first dowsing session, I never had to ask to raise his life force, his Energy level, or to adjust his body frequency. It took care of itself once the cancer frequency was scrambled, his Chakras were cleared, and his pain and immune system was addressed. This dowsing session did not make permanent changes though. It was only the beginning of his healing journey. That was only the first of many sessions. There have been more, and more remain to be done at the time of this writing. It has been a battle for this young man but as I write this, he is still strong and is touching many lives. He is fighting his battle well and we all know that everything is in order and it will continue to be in order whether his sacred contract is to be here for 14, 20, 40, or 80 years. He is healed, and healing has many meanings.

## Disease and Illness

As I stated earlier, I believe that everything has a life force and frequency including events, places, and people, past, present, and future. This, then, includes all illnesses, diseases, memories and intentions. They all vibrate at a particular frequency. This also means that they cannot survive if they are adjusted to a different frequency. The technique of dowsing allows us to tap into Universal knowledge and know what those frequencies are and how to scramble, deactivate, neutralize, and transform them if it's for the highest good. Anyone can be a healer with this kind of knowledge. Even Jesus the great Biblical teacher and healer, agrees. In Matthew 7:7–8, he said, "Ask and it shall be given to you, seek and you shall find, knock and it shall be opened to you. For EVERYONE who asks receives, and he who seeks finds, and to him who knocks it shall be opened." Well, I don't know about you, but when I am working with my pendulum, that's basically all I'm doing is asking, seeking, and knocking at the door of Universal knowledge, or my Higher Self for answers. When I ask, I receive, so can you! Because so many people have grown up reading and believing so much of the Bible, I'd like to quote a few more versus to plant deeply in your mind that you have this unlimited Power INSIDE of you. In Matthew 17:20 Jesus said, "If you have faith as a mustard seed, you shall say to this mountain (or disease, or illness, or frequency), move from here to there (be scrambled, or transformed), and it shall move (be done); and **nothing** shall be impossible to you." And one of my all time favorites is Mark 10:51. It is exactly what dowsing is all about. Jesus was working with a blind man and asked him what exactly he wanted. He knew, he asked, and he got it . . . his eye sight. If you know exactly what you want and you learn how to ask . . . you can have it. Energy is no different today than it was thousands of years ago.

If you've read any Christian scripture, you have no doubt read many healing stores. In those stories you find that it was quite common for Jesus to have people do some type of ritual before they received their healing. Sometimes he would even perform the rituals himself. One such story is when he spat on the ground and made mud to put on a blind man's eyes. Now, we know there wasn't any Power in that mud. It was the questions and intentions of Jesus and the blind man that moved the Energy in order for him to see again. But the ritual was used as a physical tool much like watching a pendulum swing. Physical signs help people believe. One more example of this is in II Kings 5:20 where Elisha told Naaman to go and wash in the Jordan River seven times in order to restore his health. It wasn't the river or the seven washing that held the Power. The Power was in the intentions. The techniques, paths, or rituals we use today are here to assist our minds, but the Power comes from "within."

Please remember that using a pendulum is only one of many paths, techniques, or rituals to build your faith and confidence.

I feel it is important to say here that I have personally experienced, on many occasions, the same powerful results without using my pendulum. There have been times when I was without my pendulum but was not willing to let that keep me from doing what I knew needed to be done. I closed my eyes and did the same dowsing process. I asked the same questions and just allowed my mind's eye to see my pendulum working. This takes a lot of practice but what it tells you is that the pendulum does not have the Power, you do. You can achieve the same amazing results with tool, techniques, or rituals as you can by simply using what you have inside. The Power!

Let's talk about what to do when you've determined that you're working with a disease or an illness.

First ask **May I dowse over this disease at this time?** If no, go to a different subject or just put your pendulum down for now. If yes, ask **What percent of _____ (the disease or illness is affecting me or the person you are working with) at this time?** Use the chart to find your answer and write the them down. Then ask **What is my (or other person's) ideal body frequency?** Then ask **What is it now?** Then ask **Is there a spirit attached to this disease or illness?** If no, move on. If yes, say **Please banish the spirit of this disease to the other side where it can no longer harm anyone.** Your pendulum will swing counterclockwise. Now say **Please scramble the frequency of** _____ **(the disease or illness).** Your pendulum will swing counterclockwise. After it has stopped, ask **What is my (or other person's) body frequency?** If it not a 100% say **Please raise my body frequency (or other person's) to 100% for my highest good. Thank you.**

## Beliefs

Beliefs are your perceptions about a given subject, and those beliefs are charged with emotions and memories. Everyone gets their beliefs from somewhere, and I believe there are three ways we acquire them.

I believe there is one of three reasons why you believe what you believe. Reason number one, I call **Childhood Conditioning.** As a young child, you simply soaked in everything you were told either by parents, adults, or a church, good or bad. Now as an adult, you have never taken the time to question any of those beliefs. You may (or may not) have been programmed with fear and guilt growing up. You may have been told that you were worthless or stupid and would never amount to anything. Maybe you have old beliefs about money that are keeping you from following your passion. Regardless of where they came from or what your old beliefs are, you simply haven't taken the time to be *aware* of what you were taught or indoctrinated with and whether it was good for you or not. You are on auto pilot.

The second reason is what I call **Controlled Conditioning.** This is when an adult agrees to live and operate by someone else's beliefs based on their personal safety, lack of self-confidence, or fear of salvation. This could be an abusive intimate relationship, kidnapping, or abusive religious brainwashing. This is when you allow yourself to be deceived by fabricated promises with an underlying tone of fear. You are led to believe that you cannot exist without them and if you tried, you would most certainly die.

The third reason is the healthiest and most empowering reason: you believe what you believe because you are **self-realized.** *Self-realization* is the *realization* that you have choices. It's when you *realize* that you do not have to live your life in fear of losing your salvation, in fear of God, or in fear of an abuser. It's when you *realize* that you can make your own decisions, have your own beliefs, and that you won't die. You *realize* that you have personal Power and you use it. You *realize* you have freedom. This personal Power comes only through taking time for inner-reflection. This isn't to say that you can't have some of the same beliefs as other people, but the difference between self-*realized* beliefs and controlled or conditioned beliefs is you are making a conscious decision for empowering beliefs based on what's best for you without judgment, fear, or guilt.

The only time I've ever seen a situation where unhappiness, unfulfillment, failure, or health problems weren't caused by a disempowering belief system is in the case of a sacred contract. Even then, I somehow think that the contract is somewhere in a person's belief system. When you change your belief system to one of empowerment, happiness, health and a life of contentment are the result. Living with an empowering belief system or a disempowering belief system is always your choice. It's now time for you to make your choice. Which do you want? If your decision is that you want an empowering belief system, let's get one for you.

Let's assume that you are suffering from constant muscle pain in your shoulders. You've tried prescription drugs and they had some effect but only until the pills wore off. Then you tried massage and found it helped for awhile too, but only for about two days and then the pain would return. Here's what I suggest. Ask **Is there an emotion or belief that is causing my shoulder pain at this time**? I venture to say your answer will be yes. What you need to do is think about what shoulders represent. I don't know if you've read or know much about the body mind connection. If you do, you know what I'm talking about here, if you haven't, there are many wonderful resources on-line and in book stores to assist you in understanding how our bodies, minds, and spirits are all connected and how we can heal ourselves by becoming *aware* of what our body is telling us. For now, I'll tell you that shoulders represent carrying burdens and experiencing joy. If your shoulders continually hurt, your body is simply trying to get your attention. Listen to it. It might be trying to tell you that you are carrying too many burdens. It might be trying to tell you it's time to take a look at what you believe about deserving and enjoying all there is in life. It might even be trying to encourage you to ask yourself whether you believe you are worthy of good things or not. Taking time to understand your body's language is one way of experiencing inner reflection and is truly one of the very best things you can do for yourself. If you take the time to do this type of work, you will find that there are disempowering beliefs somewhere in your thoughts that you're operating with and it's those beliefs that are causing your shoulder pain. Once you *realize* this, you have complete freedom to change the belief and heal yourself of the pain.

I encourage you to take the time to really tune in and listen to your body on a regular basis. It is such an amazing communicator if you will only learn to listen and understand what it's trying to tell you. But in order to "hear" what your body is saying, you need to be free of any substances that mask or numb your true emotions. You cannot feel your true emotions if you are drinking alcohol or taking prescription drugs such as anti-depressants or anti-anxiety medications. While they may give you a "feeling" that things are better in your life, they are basically numbing your emotions both the good and happy emotions as well as the depressed and hopeless emotions. Do not stop taking your medications without consulting your physician. All I'm saying is that in order to rationally evaluate and respond to your true emotions and thereby change your disempowering beliefs, you need to FEEL everything. Once you feel what's going on, you can better decide what needs to change in your belief system.

Beliefs of any type are embedded not just in your thoughts, but in your sub-conscious and unconscious minds. In fact memories, emotions, and beliefs are so powerful they are embedded at the cellular level. Your cells hold on to empowering beliefs and, unfortunately, disempowering ones as well. That's why we need to make sure to ask to remove the old beliefs from "all levels" of our existence. Each belief has a particular frequency and all frequencies create an electromagnetic field. Whatever it is you are believing or vibrating, you will draw more of that same frequency into your life and/or body. Until you change that frequency, you will continue to attract like frequencies whether they are empowering or disempowering you. If you are vibrating fear of cancer, what do you think you are attracting into your life and into your body? Cancer. If you're vibrating lack, what do you think you are attracting more of into your life? More lack. If you are vibrating compassion and kindness, what do you think you are attracting into your life? Exactly . . . more compassion and more kindness. Be mindful and *aware* of all beliefs and thoughts. What you think is what you get.

It's helpful when dowsing over your beliefs to write your thoughts and phrases down so you have a clear picture of what you're working with. It's also helpful to refer back to them occasionally to see the progress that you've made. As you take on new beliefs, I encourage you to write them out and put them where you can see them throughout your day. It helps to embed them deeper and deeper every time you see, read, and say them.

I'm a firm believer in affirmations and talk more about the amazing Power of affirmations in my book *Affirmations to Change and Heal Your Life*.

Take a little time now to ask yourself if you have any disempowering beliefs. Here are some examples:

**Do I have any disempowering beliefs about** _____ **(see following list) that need to be changed and cleared at this time?**

Religion
Salvation
God
Sex
Money
Fear
Envy
Self-Esteem
Guilt
Shame
Grief
Failure
Success
Depression
Pessimism
Intimacy
Freedom
Abandonment
Criticism
Control
Abuse
Security
Selfishness

Anger

Trust

Judgment

Everyone I have ever worked with, including myself, has had several if not many beliefs that needed to be changed. I'm sure you will, too. Here's what I want you to do: Once you have figured out what your current disempowering belief is, I want you to write it down. Then I want you to give some thought to what you would rather believe about that particular subject and write it down. What do you need to believe in order for it to empower you? Do this for as many beliefs as you need.

Now that you've written out what the old beliefs state and what you want the new belief to state, it's time to dowse over them to change the frequencies. It's very simple. The hardest part was recognizing what has been harming you, writing it down and deciding what you need to believe to be empowered.

Keep in mind that later on if you feel that a particular belief needs to change again, don't hesitate to change it. You will find that with each old belief you change you will be removing another layer of yourself. With the removal of each layer comes an *awareness* of even more beliefs that will need to be changed in order for you to continue to grow. You will find this type of personal growth can go on for a lifetime. It's all good though, for every time you remove an old disempowering belief you increase your Power.

Once you have identified the belief that needs to be changed say **Please neutralize and remove any and all emotions from the beliefs, thoughts, and memories I have concerning** _____ **(let's say unworthiness) on all levels of my existence.** Your pendulum will swing counterclockwise. While it is swinging, repeat your question over and over until it stops.

Now we need to take the Energy of that belief that has been neutralized and transform it into what you want it to be. Say **Please transform** this Energy now so that I can believe _____ ("that I deserve to enjoy all the pleasures of life and that I now deserve joy to flow freely in everything I do on all levels of my existence") or whatever is needed for my highest good. Your pendulum will swing clockwise until the Energy has transformed. While it swings, repeat your affirmation over and over.

Remember to write out the new belief or affirmation and post it where you can see it throughout the day.

You can always use the chart to see how much of your new belief has been integrated by asking **How much do I believe** _____ **(say your new belief)**?

## Example:

I believe I am capable of running and operating this business successfully.

That's your affirmation or what you want to believe. Ask **How much do I believe I am capable of running and operating this business successfully**? You'll get your number based on 100%. If it's not at 100% simply say **Please adjust my belief that I can run and operate this business successfully to 100% on all levels of my existence**. Your pendulum will swing back and forth at the current number and then gradually move to 100%.

I was working with someone a while ago who had lived with sexual humiliation for most of her life. She had been doing a lot of self reflection and was finally ready to clear her old beliefs on all levels of her existence. She had tried everything medically, including Prozac, to try to shake the affects her old beliefs had on her health and her relationships. Of course we know that prescription drugs do not change your beliefs. They may ease the symptoms of your beliefs, but only you can change your beliefs.

Here is what I did. First, I asked for permission. Second, I asked if there were any non-beneficial psychic cords attached in either direction from her or her abuser. I asked for these cords to be cut in all directions from the person who had done this to her. I then asked if there were any non beneficial frequencies involved and then for them to be scrambled. Then I asked how much she believed she deserved what had happened to her. She wasn't even *aware* at the time that she had this belief until I asked. The percentage of the old belief affecting her was huge. On some level she believed that what happened to her years ago was all her fault. Of course that's what she had been told by her abuser and she believed him. She had taken on his belief and was now operating under that spell, so to speak. The belief that she deserved or had caused what had happened to her years ago is in part what had been causing her years of bad health and harmful relationships. When she *realized* this, she was determined that it was time for that belief to go! It had a lot of Energy surrounding it and we knew it was going to take some work and thought. We also knew that the Power of our intentions was far more powerful than the old disempowering belief or spell she had been under.

I asked how much this belief was affecting her. It was 100%. I had her write her old belief down on paper. Then I asked her what she wanted her new belief to be and to write it down. I asked how much she believed her new belief. It was 0%. I asked her to hold her old belief in her hands as I asked to remove the emotions from any thoughts or memories on all levels of her existence that might be causing her to hold onto this belief. I asked to please scramble the frequencies. Then I asked to neutralize them. My pendulum swung counterclockwise so long I had to support my arm. I asked her to hold her new belief in her hands and repeat her new belief as I asked to please transform and implant this new belief on all levels of her existence for her highest good. My pendulum swung clockwise for a very long time.

We checked the percent of how much the old belief was affecting her now. It was down to from 100% to 70%. We then checked how much she believed the new belief. It went from 0% to 30%. We were making progress.

We dowsed every day until the old belief was zero and the new belief was 100%. Then we just kept placing appropriate Energy around her for a few more days. Her life has taken a new direction is all I can say!!!

I want to mention again that dowsing is only one path or technique to assist you in identifying and changing old disempowering beliefs into empowering ones. Psych-K, Brain Gems, and NET, (Neuro-Emotional Technique) are other amazing tools that may be used to remove and change old beliefs. For more information visit my Web site—http://www.pursuitofhealing.com.

# Health

When any one comes to me with a health concern, I immediately ask if their symptom is simply running its course or if there is a belief or emotion that needs to be changed at this time. Sometimes it's a simple sore throat that's causing pain. A sore throat is often the result of the immune system being run down, and a run-down immune system can be the result of a number of things including beliefs that need to be changed. Dowsing can help lower pain level and raise Energy levels but I always suggest that a person pay close attention to their symptoms, by listening to their body and making proper changes to their diet, water intake, nutritional supplement, rest, and emotional state. Dowsing is an amazing tool, but, as I've said before, there are many paths that lead to complete healing emotionally, physically, and spiritually.

If there is a belief or an emotion affecting your health; it needs to be cleared and changed. That's where you begin. You will find the steps for changing beliefs in the "Beliefs" section. I believe one hundred percent that our thoughts and emotions create our life and everything we experience in it, including all areas of our health. If you can identify the root problem and clear it, the symptoms will almost always go away. Maybe they won't go away instantly, but you will see a gradual improvement. Again, dowsing is not the only answer for this work. I am a huge supporter of acupuncture, herbs, supplements, Chiropractic, and other techniques that are available for improving overall health.

Your health is a never-ending subject as are the questions you can ask concerning it. Listed below are some of the effective questions I use when working with someone's health. They may be beneficial to you as well. You can always ask how much something is affecting you by using the chart, too.

Is there any fungus in my body?

Are there any viruses in my body?

Are there any non-beneficial bacteria in my body?

Are there any parasites in my body?

Is there any cancer present in or on my body?

Are there any tumors in or on my body?

Do I have a chemical imbalance?

Am I infected with:

    Flu

    Strep Throat

    Ecoli

    West Nile

    Bacteria of any kind

    Hepatitis of any kind

    Pneumonia

And the list goes on . . .

*Using 100% percent on the chart you can ask about the condition or levels of anything:

What is my testosterone level? Estrogen level?
To what percent is my brain chemistry balanced?
To what percent is my body chemistry balanced?
What is my serotonin level?
What is my melatonin level?
What is my thyroid level?
What is my parathyroid level?
What is my pineal level?
What is my pituitary level?
What is my body pH level?
At what level is my immune system operating?
Do I have any food allergies? Use the process of elimination.
Am I allergic to _____?
What vitamins are to my highest good? Ask by name.
How much should I take? Use the chart for numbers or hold up fingers
    one at a time until you get a yes.

Ask if you have any problems that need to be addressed concerning anything:

Lymph Glands
Adrenal Glands
Prostate
Ovaries
Spleen
Heart
Kidney
Liver
Gall Bladder

Pancreas
Digestive Tract
Skeletal Alignment
Tendons
Ligaments
Bones
Bone Density
Nervous System
And the list goes on . . .

Am I being negatively affected by any:

Chemicals I use or that I am around
Food preservatives
Inhalants
Pollutants
Electrical Lines
Radiation

Is it to my highest good to seek out _____ at this time?
Who? Go through names.

Chiropractic treatment
Naturopathic Doctor
  Medical Doctor
  Physical Therapy
  Massage therapist
Acupuncturist
Counseling
Hypnotherapy

Is it to my highest good to incorporate _____ into my life?

Herbs
Flower Essence
Aromatherapy
Meditation
Yoga
Affirmations
A particular medication

Dowsing also works extremely well on someone who is wanting to lose weight. The results I've seen are simply amazing. The first thing I do when working with someone who wants to lose weight is to put them on a fitness and nutritional program. Then, if they are open to dowsing, I add it to their program.

I begin my questions by asking **What is** _____ **(the person's) ideal weight?** If it's important to them, I ask **What is their ideal size?** I use the chart to get their answers. These numbers then become their goal. What's so great about knowing this information is that they know they have the ability to achieve their goal because it's their ideal weight and size.

When coaching people for weight loss, I find we almost always end up doing a lot of belief changing work. We all know how easy it is to eat because of emotional triggers whether those emotions are self sabotage, sadness or loneliness. Once we clear and change some of their old beliefs into new ones, the person usually begins to make better choices, take better care of himself/herself, and the weight begin to come off more easily and much faster. On a few occasions I have found negative Energy or entities that are causing the person to overeat or binge, upsetting the body frequency. Desired results may not come after just one session, but I encourage people to continue; results *will* come. Each time I work with someone, I say **Please place the most appropriate Energy around _____ (the person) as they make changes in their life so they may reach their ideal weight and size and maintain it with ease.** My pendulum swings clockwise.

Affirmations are extremely important in all areas of your life and especially when you're pursuing better health. For more information about affirmations see my Web site or pick up my book, *Affirmations to Change and Heal Your Life*.

## Food and Water

Sometimes it is impossible to have access to clean water and food. On those rare occasions I have found that setting my intentions and dowsing over the food and water I consume has saved me more than once from spending time in the bathroom like many of my friends have had to do. Once they found out what I was doing, I began dowsing for them as well until they learned to do it for themselves. This is just another example of the unlimited resource that is available to us if we just remember to tap into it and ask the right questions.

Dowsing is also helpful when shopping for foods containing the highest Energy levels. Don't be afraid to ask what stores have the safest and freshest produce, meat, fish, and dairy. Use the process of elimination to find your answer. I found this helpful when the big bottled water controversy came out. I simply asked which of the bottled water companies had the safest water. Now I know and you can, too.

## Prosperity

Yes, even prosperity has a frequency. Prosperity can be a very complex subject because it has so many beliefs attached to it. Haven't you heard people say that "money is the root of all evil" or "you have to work your fingers to the bone to get ahead"? Well those people probably do have to work their fingers to the bone because that's what they believe about prosperity. They vibrate their belief. And if their belief is that they have to work their fingers to the bone then that's what they'll vibrate, attract, and experience. Unless they change their belief to something like "money flows easily into my life," they will not vibrate the flow of money and they certainly will not attract the flow of money.

So here's what you do to adjust your frequencies to resonate with those of prosperity. Using the chart, ask **What is my prosperity level?** If it's 100%, you're fine. If it's below 100%, ask **Do I have any resistance to receiving prosperity into my life?** If you do, say **Please neutralize any resistance I may have about receiving prosperity into my life.** Your pendulum will swing counterclockwise. Then say **Please adjust my frequencies to that of prosperity for my highest good.** Your pendulum will swing clockwise.

If your prosperity level does not stay at 100% and you find that you have to dowse over it often, or if you are not experiencing the changes that you expect, refer to the "Beliefs" section and work on your beliefs about money and prosperity. As with any area you dowse over, if it doesn't stay fairly consistent, peel off another layer and go a little deeper. "Beliefs" is usually where you will end up. And that's a good thing.

## Relationships

You most definitely can use dowsing to ease problems in relationships. As you've already read, psychic cords are usually involved in unhealthy or deteriorating relationships and that's a good place to begin your work. If you ever encounter a situation where someone simply hates you, just remember: you cannot change them; you can only change yourself. BUT you *can* change the flow and frequencies of the Energy surrounding your circumstances.

For struggling relationship situations, I always begin by asking permission, then by asking **What is the compatibility level between _____ (the person) and myself?** Use the chart to get your percentage based on 100%.

Then ask **Are there any non-beneficial frequencies between _____ (person) and me?** If there are, say **Please scramble any and all non-beneficial frequencies on all levels of our existence past, present, and future, for our highest good.** I say this because sometimes a person hates you or you them without knowing why. It could be possible that you had experiences from another lifetime and those frequencies have been carried over. Saying "on all levels" covers all your bases. Your pendulum will swing counterclockwise. Now say **Please transform this Energy into the most appropriate Energy to the highest good for both of us.** Your pendulum will swing clockwise. Check your compatibility level again. It should be much better if not 100%.

If you are *aware* of what the problem is between the two of you, you can consult the "Beliefs" section and work on changing emotions, thoughts, and memories you may have about one another. If you're not *aware* of the beliefs but know they're there, simply say **Please remove any and all emotions affecting the beliefs, thoughts, and memories we have about one another on all levels of our existence past, present, and future, to our highest good.** Your pendulum will swing counterclockwise. Then say **Please transform this Energy into the most appropriate Energy for both our highest good.**

As you can see, your options are endless.

Check compatibility levels when you are interviewing or hiring someone. Check it on your family, doctors, teachers, and businesses. This is extremely helpful in making any kind of decision. If it isn't 100%, go through the steps or simply say **Please raise the compatibility level of my family for our highest good.** Doing this though, without peeling off layers in order to find out why your family is hav-ing problems, is a bit like treating a physical symptom instead of the problem. Don't ignore the problem. Take the time to find out why your family is having problems and address them. If you do that, your compatibility level will rise on its own. But if you're in a crisis, on vacation, or just need that quick shift, by all means, take this shortcut and change the Energy.

# CHAPTER 5

# More Examples

O ver the course of a couple years I remodeled several houses and condos in the mountains of Colorado. Throughout the process I used my pendulum to help me with all types of decisions including finding contractors, making choices for colors, fabrics, furniture, even appliances. It certainly made the process much more pleasant. One of my most enjoyable experiences came while I was shopping for furniture in Denver. I had forgotten my carpet sample back at the mountain house and I really did need it. I was trying to match beige colors and you know how many shades there are of beige. They go from pink, to yellow, to green. Well, I pulled out my pendulum and began to ask questions like: Will this sofa color match the paint and carpet in this particular house? If I got a no, I moved on. If I got a yes, I added it to my list of sofas that would definitely match. I found three or four sofas with a yes answer. Then I proceeded to eliminate one at a time by asking the right questions until I found the perfect sofa. And yes, it matches perfectly! I had no doubt.

Another great use for dowsing is when you're planning a vacation. I've used it to decide where to go, when to go and where to stay. It's all in the way you ask the questions.

When dowsing for answers, make sure to think beyond just the question, though. Here's what I mean: I do a lot of flying in a private plane and most of my flying is in the mountains of Colorado. As you can imagine, the weather can be a little intense with snow and ice and mountain updrafts and downdrafts. When I first began to ask questions about the weather I quickly learned I wasn't asking correctly. On one particular occasion and before I knew better, I asked if the weather would be good on Friday. My answer was yes, so I was all relaxed until it was time to get into the plane and fly. There was an incredible snow storm where I was planning to land. Instead of doubting the pendulum, I stopped and asked myself what I had done wrong. As I thought about it, I began to *realize* that my question was too vague. I asked **Will the weather be good on Friday?** Well, good for whom? Skiers or pilots? Woops. That Friday was an awesome day for skiers because it was snowing like crazy. On the other hand, it was not a good day for pilots. I learned quickly that questions need to be precise and detailed in order to get clear helpful answers. I learned that I really need to think about all angles. So now I ask: will the weather be clear and smooth for flying on Friday? Do you see the difference? The other way I ask is: is it to my highest good to fly on Friday?

Not too long ago, someone very close to me asked me to dowse for her concerning her heart. She had been under quite a lot of emotional stress and her heart was giving her some problems. We stole away to the mountains for a couple days of downtime. We methodically formed our questions and then began our work. We found that she was in need of not only emotional clearing but also physical detoxification. During those two days, we cleared major old beliefs and emotions. At the same time, her physical body went through major clearing as well. I'm talking about *natural* cleansing. She didn't take any pills or drink anything that would cause her system to cleanse the way it did. It was the Energy work that caused her to detoxify. Immediately her heart palpitations ceased, her breathing was easier, and she never did take any of her prescribed medications. It was awesome! This does not mean you should stop taking your medication for any reason without consulting your doctor.

My stories are endless, and yours will be, too. I hope the few I have shared with you have been helpful in awakening you and helping you *realize* that you have unlimited abilities and opportunities available to you if you are only open to them and willing to do a little work. As with anything in this life, you always get out of it what you put into it. You will find that dowsing is no different.

As you master the art of dowsing, please remember to be mindful and respectful of the unlimited information you have access to. Always ask if the time is appropriate and if you have permission to continue. Make sure that you do not ask a question if you don't really want to know the answer or if you're not sure you can handle the responsibility of knowing it. As you are given more and more information you are also given more and more responsibility in managing that information. And finally, always work for the highest good of everyone involved. Without exception!

Here is to your continued pursuit of healing—emotionally, physically, and spiritually.

# About the Author

For nearly thirty years, Vicky Thurlow has inspired tens of thousands of individuals with her passion for life. As a certified fitness instructor, personal trainer, model, author, entrepreneur and business owner, she fully understands the importance of discipline, fitness, and beauty from the inside out.

Overcoming her cult-like religious upbringing and battling a medically incurable condition, Vicky's unrelenting desire to heal herself and help others enabled her to successfully learn to trust holistic healing techniques, and change her life forever. She energetically lives her purpose and openly shares her experiences to help others connect to an array of healing techniques and resources.

For more information about Vicky's work, books, guided meditations, CDs, DVDs, workshops, and healing resources, please visit her Web site: http://www.pursuitofhealing.com.

# TO PURCHASE ADDITIONAL COPIES OF THIS BOOK

Contact DVT Investments
2800 Printers Way,
Grand Junction, Colorado 81506

or visit http://www.pursuitofhealing.com

# NOTES

# NOTES

# NOTES

# NOTES

# NOTES